THE BANTING DIET

TASTY RECIPES

MARGARET T. HASHIMOTO

CONTENTS

CHAPTER ONE
WHAT IS THE BANTING DIET AND HOW DOES IT WORK?

The Banting diet, named after its creator William Banting, is a low-carbohydrate, high-fat diet. The theory behind this diet is that eating a diet high in fat and low in carbohydrates causes your body to switch from burning carbohydrates to burning fat for energy. For a variety of reasons, the diet is extremely effective, particularly for people who are carbohydrate intolerant.

• If you gain weight around your waist rather than your thighs, you may be carbohydrate intolerant.

• If sugary or starchy foods make you feel sluggish.

• If you wake up with a strong desire to eat.

• If you're a picky eater.

• If you gain weight more quickly than your friends or family.

• If your weight changes.

• If you have any of the above symptoms, the Banting Diet may be able to help you.

• The Banting Diet gives you a general sense of well-being and drastically reduces stress, resulting in better sleep.

• Cravings for food begin to fade. This is due to the fact that fat has been shown to make you feel fuller for longer.

The process of losing weight starts almost immediately. • Being able to eat the foods you thought were bad for you while still losing weight is what Banting is all about.

• Avoiding high-processed foods like sugars and refined grains.

CHAPTER TWO
ANIMAL FAT IS GOOD FOR YOU.

Notes on the Banting Diet

The Banting Diet revolves around this. Because we've always been taught that fat makes us fat, this throws us for a loop. Sugar and refined carbs cause insulin spikes, which tell your body to store energy as fat.

Eat as many vegetables as possible.

All Banters refer to vegetables as 'bulk food.' Green vegetables are the go-to vegetables, and everyone knows that eating a variety of them is good for the body.

Snacking is strictly forbidden unless it is Banting Friendly.

Snacking is considered a form of cheating, especially during the first week of the Banting diet. If you want to snack, make sure it's Banting-friendly. Increase your intake of animal fat, which acts as a natural appetite suppressant, to beat those hunger pangs.

Never deceive yourself about anything.

Consuming high carbohydrate foods can be found in peanuts, baked beans, and legumes. To make sure you're following the rules, consult the "Banting Diet red list; foods that should not be consumed as a Banter."

Never overeat or undereat.

CHAPTER THREE

BEGINNER BANTERS

Beginner Banters have a habit of either overeating or undereating. You can't eat as much fat as you want just because you're on a low-carb diet. After all, if you consume more calories than you expend, you will gain weight.

On the other hand, if you're on the Banting Diet, don't go hungry. Because fat contains fewer calories than carbohydrates, you'll probably need to eat more than you think. If you're interested in learning more,

If you become extremely hungry while on the Banting diet, it's likely that you're either undereating or not eating enough fat. The great thing about this diet is that fat is much more filling than carbohydrates, so you shouldn't be hungry at all if you follow it correctly.

Don't eat too much protein.

The Banting diet is a low-carb, high-fat diet, not a high-protein diet. The Banting Diet's main goal is to eliminate carbohydrates from your diet and replace them with more fat. Don't put too much emphasis on increasing your protein intake. With all of the vegetables and meat you'll be eating, you'll get enough protein naturally.

Always read the labels on your food.

When it comes to ready-to-eat meals or processed foods, always be on the lookout. Carbohydrates are almost always found in these foods. Avoid foods that claim to be low in fat. Although these foods are low in fat, the fats have been replaced with sugars in order to compensate for the flavor loss. "Low Fat Meals" are nothing more than a clever marketing ploy.

CHAPTER FOUR

DON'T EAT TOO MANY FRUITS AND NUTS.

Natural fructose, also known as "nature's sugar," can be found in fruits. Sugar should be limited, if not avoided entirely, on the Banting diet.

Nuts are on the Banting Diet's green list, but like any other food, they should be consumed in moderation. People tend to overeat nuts because they are such a convenient snack to have with them all day.

Limit your dairy intake.

Dairy does contain carbohydrates, and while this can be beneficial to the body, it should be consumed in moderation. Dairy does contain a small amount of carbohydrates, so it's not a carb-free zone. If you're lactose intolerant, stay away from dairy completely.

Maintain your fortitude.

When it comes to the Banting Diet, a lot of people give up too soon. Because your body is still working to get rid of those nasty carb cravings, the first ten days of any diet are always the most difficult. Stick with it for 10 days, and you'll notice significant changes in your weight and mood.

CHAPTER FIVE

THE BANTING DIET: HOW TO FOLLOW IT

The Banting diet is divided into four phases to make the transition to an LCHF lifestyle as painless as possible.

While the diet can be followed on your own, those who want a structured and personalized Banting meal plan can enroll in an online course.

To help manage temptations and make the transition easier, the course includes a step-by-step guide, recipes, optional daily coaching, and weekly mindset workshops.

Observation (Phase 1)

During this one-week period, you should stick to your current diet with no changes.

It encourages you to keep track of everything you eat and write about it in order to figure out how you react to food.

CHAPTER SIX

RESTORATION

The restoration phase is designed to help you reclaim your gut health and acclimate to the Banting diet.

Depending on your weight-loss goal, this phase may last 2–12 weeks. In general, for every 11 pounds (5 kg) of weight you want to lose, you should follow it for one week.

You'll be given a series of food lists to look at during this time. All foods on the Red and Light Red lists should be avoided, and only foods on the Green and Orange lists should be consumed.

This phase has the benefit of not requiring calorie counting or portion control.

Transformation is the final phase.

The original Banting diet is introduced in the transformation phase.

It takes your new eating habits and reduces your carb intake to put you in ketosis, which is a fat-burning state.

To achieve this, the method encourages you to eat foods from the Green list, while adding foods from the Orange list — as well as the Red lists previously mentioned — to the no-go foods list.

This third phase lasts as long as it takes you to reach your goal weight, and you should keep track of your meals every two weeks for a couple of days.

In order to avoid hitting a weight-loss plateau, the phase also includes "lifestyle hacks" like intermittent fasting, exercise tips, sleep and meditation.

The transformation phase is supposed to help with mental clarity, sleep, acne, skin irritations, and even joint pain.

CHAPTER SEVEN

PRESERVATION

Once you've reached your desired weight, you'll enter the final phase, which is meant to last indefinitely. Its purpose is to assist you in maintaining your new weight over time.

This is a more flexible phase because you'll be able to reintroduce foods that were previously prohibited. The goal is to figure out which ones you can eat without gaining weight while doing so.

During this phase, there is no food tracking, and you may use the following food lists:

• No restrictions: green

• Eat in moderation if you're eating oranges.

• Light Red: only worn on rare occasions or for special occasions.

• Never (red)

• Gray: you make the decision.

If you feel like you have lost control of your weight, you can always return to the previous phase.

When following the Banting diet, is it possible to develop gallstones?

No, but if you already have gallstones, you'll feel some discomfort in the short term.

Is the Banting Diet suitable for all types of people?

Yes, people who follow the Banting Diet have little trouble keeping their weight under control. People who consume a lot of carbohydrates, on the other hand, have a hard time staying in shape.

Is the Banting Diet right for you?

The Banting Diet has shown to be effective for people with Type 2 Diabetes, Hypercholesterolemia, Obesity, Hypertension, and anyone struggling to maintain a healthy weight.

Is it necessary to keep track of your calories and carbs when you're on the Banting diet?

Calorie counting isn't necessary. You should be able to stay within the guidelines if you stick to the green items on the list. Carbohydrate intake, on the other hand, should be limited. Reduce your carb intake if you aren't losing weight.

Is it necessary for me to exercise while following the Banting diet?

Yes. Even if it's only for 10 to 15 minutes a day, we always recommend exercising. Exercising has numerous advantages, including the ability to help you lose weight.

Is the Banting Diet suitable for kids?

Yes. Sugary foods are not good for anyone's health. The Banting Diet should be considered if your child is struggling with their weight.

Is there any side effects to the Banting Diet?

Yes, but the negative effects are only temporary. The Banting Diet may cause dizziness, abdominal cramps, muscle pain, shivers, and sweats in its early stages. However, as your body adjusts to the diet, you should feel even better than you did before you began.

Is there any evidence that the Banting Diet works for weight loss?

Yes, it works wonders. You can control your blood glucose and insulin levels by eating low carbs, which aids in fat burning. Reducing your carbohydrate intake can help you control your sweet and starchy food cravings. A low-carbohydrate diet is the only way to accomplish this.

Is it permissible to consume fat on the Banting Diet?

Yes! Yes! Yes! Yes! Yes! Yes! Yes! Yes! Yes! Yes Saturated fat is not linked to heart disease, according to research. This is supported by a large body of evidence.

Animal protein is good for you.

• Eggs

- Offal

- Poultry

- Meats

- Cured meats that have been left to age naturally

- Seafood

Vegetables:

- Cauliflower

- Lettuce

- Avocados

- Broccoli

- Sauerkraut

- Tomatoes

- Spinach

- Aubergines

- Cabbage

- Onion (spring)

- Leeks

- Onions

- Pumpkins

Artichoke hearts are a type of artichoke that has a heart

- Radishes

- Asparagus

- Mushrooms

- Olives

- Courgettes

Dairy:

• Milk with all of the cream

• Cheesy cottage

• Dairy products

• Cream

• Greek yoghurt with the full cream

• Cheeses that are not hard

• Cheesy snacks

Fats:

• Animal fat, rendered

Macadamia oil is a type of oil that comes from macadamia nuts

• Almonds

• Oil extracted from avocado

Nuts and seeds are two of the most nutritious foods you can eat.

• Flaxseeds

Seeds of sunflower

• Sweeteners

• Butter

• Oil made from coconut

• Nuts of pine

• Walnuts

• Lard

• Cheese

• Full-fat mayonnaise

Seeds from pumpkin

• granules of erythritol

Macadamia nuts are a type of nut that is native to Australia.

• Fat from ducks

• Ghee

• Nuts of pecan

condiments and flavorings

• All flavors and condiments are acceptable as long as they are free of sugars, preservatives, and vegetable oils.

Fruits: Fruits are a good way to cut down on calories.

• Blueberries

• Quinces

• Honey

• Watermelon

• Blackberries

• Raspberries

• Nuts

• Peaches

• Bananas

• Vegetables

• Cashews

• Mangos

• Carrots

kiwis

• Nectarines

• Pawpaw

• Chestnuts

• Clementines

• 1 sliced pineapple

- Sweeteners

- Sweet potato

- Figs

- Oranges

- Gooseberries

- Guavas

- Pears

- Litchis

- Plums

- Grapes (green) under

- Prickly pears

- Cherries

- Pomegranate

• Strawberries

• Apples

• Butternut

Food to avoid Baked goods:

• Pastas, noodles

• Rice

• Beans

• All grains - wheat, oats, barley, rye

• Sorghum

• Rice cakes

• Millet

• Breakfast cereals, muesli, granola of any kind

• Brans

- Couscous

- Breaded or battered foods

- All flours from grains, wheat flour, cornflour, rye flour, barley flour, pea flour, rice flour

- All forms of bread

- Buckwheat

- Crackers, cracker breads

- Corn products - popcorn, polenta, corn thins, maize

- Cakes, biscuits, confectionary

Thickening agents:

- Gravy powder

- Stock cubes

- Maize starch Beverages: • Fizzy drinks of any description other than carbonated water

• Beer

• Diet drinks of any description

• Cider

Dairy / dairy-related:

• Rice milk

• Cheese spreads, commercial spreads

• Puddings

• Fat-free anything

• Commercial almond milk

• Ice cream

• Coffee creamers

• Reduced-fat cow's milk

• Soy milk

• Condensed milk

Fats:

• All seed oils

• Margarine

• Vegetable oils

• Chocolate

• Marinades

• Salad dressings

• Vegetable fats

Fruits and vegetables:

• Any type of fruit juice

• Vegetable juices

General:

• All fast food

• All processed food

• Any food with added sugar such as glucose, dextrose

Meat:

• All unfermented soya

• All processed meats

• Meats cured with excessive sugar

• Vienna sausages, luncheon meats

Sweeteners:

• Agave anything

• Cordials

• Malt

• Dried fruit

• Artificial sweeteners

• Fructose

• Honey

• Syrups of any kind

• Sugar

Meal plan for the Banting diet.

Monday\sBreakfast

• 2 eggs (fried) (fried)

• Few rashers of bacon or pork sausage

• Tomato Lunch • Large salad with steak or chicken and cottage cheese Snack\s• Apple slices with almond butter Dinner\s• Beef with steamed spinach and pumpkin and a small tub of Greek yoghurt

Tuesday\sBreakfast

• Omelette with bacon, cheese, rocket and tomato Lunch\s• Sautéed vegetables Snack\s• Small can of tuna Dinner\s• Greek salad with olive oil

• Broccoli or cauliflower with cream cheese

• Steak

Wednesday\sBreakfast

• Eggs and bacon

• Coconut milk smoothie Lunch • Green leafy salad

• Chicken breast Snack\s• Yoghurt Dinner\s• Roast chicken

• Pumpkin with butter

• Baby marrow with cheese sprinkled on top

Thursday\sBreakfast

• Scrambled eggs in butter

• Few rashers bacon

• Mushrooms, onions, tomato and pepper friend in bacon fat
Lunch\s• Biltong salad with full cream yoghurt Snack

• Hard boiled eggs

CHAPTER EIGHT

DINNER

- Fish and some prawns

- Spinach and pumpkin and a Greek salad

Friday\sBreakfast

- Banana pancakes

- Coconut smoothie Lunch\s• Vegetable soup Snack\s• Biltong Dinner\s• Beef or chicken

- Stir fried vegetables in olive oil

Saturday\sBreakfast

• Yoghurt and berries smoothie Lunch\s• Egg and sweet potato hash browns Snack\s• Mixed raw nuts Dinner\s• Hake friend in butter and lemon juice

• Spinach with butter and garlic

• Grilled pumpkin

Sunday\sBreakfast

• Eggs

• Bacon

• Mushrooms fried in olive oil Lunch\s• ¼ chicken

• Cucumber and tomato slices Snack\s• Avocado Dinner\s• Steak

• Roasted butternut

• Spinach

Recipes for Banting

CHICKEN SOUP FOR THE SOUL\sPreparation time 1 hour 10 minutes

Ingredients

• 400 g chicken thighs (boneless and thinly sliced) (boneless and thinly sliced)

• 1 medium stalk celery (cut into bite sized chunks)

• 3 thick leeks (sliced into thick discs) (sliced into thick discs)

• 1 large carrot (cut in half lengthways and then into 1cm thick pieces) (cut in half lengthways and then into 1cm thick pieces)

• 1 whole bay leaf

• 1 pinch salt and black pepper

• 1 handful italian parsley (roughly chopped) (roughly chopped)

• 50 ml lemon juice

• 1 l chicken stock

CHAPTER NINE

RECIPE I

Instructions

1. Place everything apart from the seasoning, parsley and lemon juice into a medium pot.

2. Pump the heat up until it hits a rolling boil, then drop it down to a gentle simmer.

3. Leave it like that for about an hour, topping up with water if it reduces too much (only top it up to the level at which you started, otherwise you'll dilute it).

4. By this point the chicken should be tender and the vegetables should be soft.

5. Add the parsley and lemon juice and season with salt and pepper to taste and serve.

GAME FISH TIRADITO Preparation time 15 minutes Instructions • 500 g barramundi, yellowtail or yellowfin tuna fillet (boned and skinned)

• 125 ml lime juice (juice of 5 limes)

• 1 whole red chilli (finely chopped)

• 1 tsp amarillo paste (or any medium strength chilli paste)

• 1 clove garlic (diced) (diced)

• 4 tbsp extra virgin olive oil

• ½ handful fresh coriander (roughly chopped)

• 1 tbsp black sesame seeds (toasted)

• 1 tbsp white sesame seeds (toasted)

• 1 pinch salt and pepper (to taste) (to taste)

CHAPTER TEN

RECIPE 2

Instructions

1. Blitz the lime juice, chilli, amarillo paste, garlic and oil in a small jug with a stick blender.

2. Mix through the coriander and season to taste with salt and pepper.

3. Slice the fish into neat sashimi-style slices and lay them neatly on a serving dish.

4. Pour the tiradito marinade over the fish and pepper with sesame seeds and any leftover

coriander.

OKRA CHARRED WITH CORIANDER AND LEMON DRESSING

Preparation time 11 minutes

Ingredients

• 300 g okra

• 4 tbsp extra virgin olive oil

• 40 ml lemon juice (juice and zest of a big fat juicey lemon)

• ¼ medium red onion (super-finely chopped)

• 1 clove garlic (minced)

• ½ whole red chilli (finely chopped)

• ½ handful coriander (roughly chopped)

CHAPTER ELEVEN

RECIPE 3

Instructions

1. Get your BBQ up to a medium heat then make the dressing.

2. Whisk the olive oil, lemon juice and zest, onion, garlic, chilli and coriander together in a large mixing bowl and season with salt and pepper.

3. Place the okra on the grill or flame for 3 minutes on each side until evenly charred.

4. While they're still hot, add the okra to the dressing and toss them to suck up the dressing.

5. Tip them onto a platter and serve hot or cold.

CHAPTER TWELVE

RECIPE 4

PORK RAMEN WITHOUT THE RAMEN (RAMEN WITHOUT THE RAMEN)

Preparation time 1 hour

Ingredients

- 1 tsp sesame oil

- 80 ml soy sauce

- 2 cloves garlic (thinly sliced)

- 500 g pork steaks

- 2 tsp coconut oil

- 2 tsp ginger (finely grated)

- 1 tsp chinese five spice

- 1 whole red chilli (finely sliced)

- 1 ½ l basic pork broth

- 250 ml water

- 200 g button mushrooms (quartered)

- 150 g mange tout (halved)

- 2 large medium-boiled eggs (cut lengthways)

- 200 g bean sprouts

- 50 g sesame seeds (toasted)

CHAPTER THIRTEEN

RECIPE 5

Instructions

1. For the pork marinade, combine the sesame oil, half of the soy sauce and half of the garlic in a mixing bowl.

2. Add the pork steaks, mix them together and leave them to marinate for 20 minutes.

3. Heat the coconut oil in a large saucepan over medium heat and add the ginger, five spice, chilli and remaining garlic, and cook for 2 minutes until they become aromatic.

4. Now add the pork broth, water and remaining soy sauce and bring it to the boil.

5. Once it begins to boil, reduce the heat and leave to simmer for 15 minutes.

6. Meanwhile, get a griddle pan very hot and grill the pork steaks for 3 minutes on each side. Leave them to rest before cutting them into strips.

7. Back to the broth, assuming 15 minutes have passed, add the mushrooms and mange tout and cook until tender.

8. To serve, divide the bean sprouts among serving bowls. Place the sliced pork and egg on top of the sprouts, fill each bowl with the broth. Finish it off with a sprinkling of sesame seeds.

TAHINI DRESSED GREEK KALE SALAD

Preparation time 10 minutes

Ingredients

• 200 g kale (destemmed and cut into big strips)

• ½ tsp fine salt

• ½ cup kalamata olives (pitted and thinly sliced)

- ⅓ cup sun-dried tomatoes (olive oil packed, rinsed and drained)

- ⅓ cup parmesan cheese (grated)

- ¼ cup sunflower seeds (toasted)

- 1 tbsp extra virgin olive oil

- ¼ cup tahini

- 80 ml lemon juice (juice of 2 lemons)

- 1 clove garlic (minced)

- ½ tsp dijon mustard

- 30 ml water

- 1 pinch salt and black pepper

CHAPTER FOURTEEN

RECIPE 6

Instructions

1. Place the kale in a bowl and massage the leaves with 1 tsp of fine salt until the leaves go darker in colour and look bruised.

2. Now, add the remaining ingredients and mix gently until the all of the ingredients have a good coating of dressing

3. Serve immediately.

NUTTY SAGEY GEM SQUASH PUREE Preparation time 20 minutes

Ingredients

• 4 large gem squash (steamed and seeded - flesh only)

• 3 tbsp butter

• ½ cup cream

• 10 big leaves of sage (shredded)

• 1 pinch salt and black pepper

CHAPTER FIFTEEN

RECIPE 7

Instructions

1. Melt the butter in a medium pot and get it hot until it goes nutty brown.

2. The moment it turns brown, add the sage and stir it in as it crackles and spits

3. Quickly add the cream and bring it to the boil then simmer it gently until it reduces by half.

4. Now add the flesh of the squash, crushing and stirring it gently with a wooden spoon over the heat until the cream and the moisture dry up and the mix is thick and holding its shape.

5. Season it with salt and pepper to taste and serve immediately.

BACON ONIONS WITH A CREAMY FLAVOR

Preparation time 1 hour 20 minutes

Ingredients

• 2 medium onions (topped, tailed, peeled and halved)

• 8 rashers streaky bacon

• 4 tbsp extra virgin olive oil

• 2 tsp thyme leaves (chopped)

• 1 cup beef stock (or broth)

• ½ cup cream

• ½ cup parmesan (grated)

• 1 pinch salt and black pepper

CHAPTER SIXTEEN

RECIPE 8

Instructions

1. Preheat the oven to 180.

2. Get the oil hot in a large pan and add the onions. Leave them to go dark brown on one side before turning them. Once they are brown, remove them from the heat.

3. In a bowl, whisk together the beef broth and cream.

4. Wrap the rashers around the onions, pinning them with toothpicks to stay in place, and pack

them tightly in a lasagne dish.

5. Pour the cream mixture around them and give the onions a drizzle of olive oil, a sprinkling of thyme, and some salt and pepper.

6. Now roast them for 40 minutes, uncovered.

7. Before serving, top each onion with some grated parmesan and bang them back in the oven either under the grill, or at a high heat to get that cheese golden and gooey.

OLIVES AND TOMATOES IN A PAN FRIED HADDOCK

Preparation time 20 minutes

Ingredients

• 4 fillet fresh haddock fillets (roughly 180g each)

• ½ cup extra virgin olive oil

• 1 medium onion (finely chopped)

• 2 cloves garlic (minced)

• ⅓ cup dry white wine

- ½ cup cherry tomatoes (halved)

- ¼ cup black olives (pitted)

- ¼ cup chicken broth

- ¼ cup flat-leaf parsley (chopped)

- ½ cup handful fresh basil (chopped)

- 1 pinch salt and black pepper

CHAPTER SEVENTEEN

RECIPE 9

Instructions

1. Season the fillets liberally with salt and pepper.

2. Heat half the olive oil in a large pan and add the fillets to cook for 4 minutes on each side, then

set them aside.

3. Add the remaining olive oil to the same pan and add the onion to sauté until it starts to caramelise, then add the add the garlic and keep stirring until it gets fragrant.

4.

Add the wine and use your wooden spoon to scrape the particles loose from the bottom of the pan.

5.

Once the wine has reduced by half, add the tomatoes, olives and capers and cook them until the wine has dried up.

6.

Now, whisk in the chicken stock and allow it decrease by half before checking the seasoning and mixing in the parsley and basil.

7.

Finally, return the fish to the pan and continue to ladle the sauce over it until it is well warmed.

CAULIFLOWER, WHOLE, ROASTED JERK

Preparation time 45 minutes

Ingredients

• 1 cauliflower head (trimmed of leaves and stemmed)

- 2 tbsp salt

- 2 tsp onion powder

- 2 tsp ground allspice

- 2 tsp garlic powder

- 1 tsp dried red chillies

- 1 tsp black pepper

- 1 tsp ground nutmeg

- 1 tsp dried chives

- 1 tsp paprika

- 1 tsp ground ginger

- ½ tsp dried thyme

- ½ tsp ground cloves

- ½ tsp ground cinnamon

- 2 tbsp coconut oil (melted) (melted)

- 1 big lemon (cut into wedges) (cut into wedges)

Chapter Eighteen

RECIPE 10

Instructions

1.

Preheat the oven to 180 degrees Celsius.

2.

Rub the oil and jerk spice all over it until it's evenly covered.

3.

Place the head on a baking sheet and cover with foil.

4.

Cook it for 1 hour with the foil on, then uncover it and roast for another 20 minutes. It should be almost black in color.

5.

Serve with lemon wedges right out of the oven.

HADDOCK, CHEDDAR, AND SPINACH EGGS IN THE BAKING PAN

Time to prepare: 35 minutes

Ingredients

• a little amount of butter to grease the pan

• 1 tablespoon of butter

• 80 g spinach (baby)

• 100 g cheddar cheese, grated

• 4 tablespoons cream

• a smidgeon of nutmeg

• 200 g smoked haddock, chunked

• A total of 8 eggs

CHAPTER NINETEEN

RECIPE II

Instructions

1.

Preheat the oven to 180 degrees Celsius.

2.

Using a considerable quantity of butter, grease four large ramekins, enamel cups, or ovenproof bowls.

3.

Heat the butter in a frying pan and cook the spinach until it has wilted. Remove the spinach from the heat and squeeze off any remaining liquid.

4.

Break two eggs into each ramekin and divide the spinach and haddock amongst them. Add a tablespoon of cream, a dash of nutmeg, and some shredded cheese to the eggs. Season with salt and pepper to taste.

5.

Bake for 15–20 minutes, or until the eggs are fully cooked and golden brown on top. With a squeeze of lemon, serve right away.

TOAST WITH COCONUT

Time to prepare: 15 minutes

Ingredients

• 2 whisked eggs

• 2 slices coconut banting bread

• 2 tablespoons butter (for frying)

- berry compote or coulis

- 14 cup berries (your favourite)

- xylitol, 2 tbsp

- to be served with

- 1 tablespoon of berry coulis

- 14 cup greek yoghurt (double thick)

- 6 almonds, whole and raw, coarsely chopped

CHAPTER TWENTY

RECIPE 12

Instructions

1.

Place the eggs in a flat basin and whisk them well.

2.

Heat the butter in a frying skillet over medium heat.

3.

Soak the bread for a few seconds on each side in the egg mixture, so that the egg is sucked out.

into the loaf of bread

4.

Fry the bread until both sides are browned.

5.

To prepare the coulis/compote, combine the berries and xylitol in a saucepan and heat to a low simmer (the berries should release their own juice, so no need to add water). Leave the berries whole for a compote. Simply purée the contents in a food processor or with a stick blender to make a coulis.

6.

Serve with the coulis, almonds, and yoghurt on the side.

SQUEAKY KASSLER CHOPS

Time to prepare: 50 minutes

Ingredients

• 2 kassler pork chops, smoked

- 2 tablespoons butter (for frying)

- for the squeak and bubble

- 2 tablespoons butter

- 1 sliced onion

- 1 garlic clove, minced

- 3 cups shredded cabbage

- 100 g florets of cauliflower

- a pinch of salt and pepper

Chapter Twenty-One

RECIPE 13

To make the sauce

• Cream (150 mL)

• 1 tbsp mustard (dijon)

• 1 tablespoon mustard (wholegrain)

Instructions

1.

To make the chops, melt the butter in a frying pan and fry the chops on both sides until golden. Each side should take roughly 5 minutes.

2.

Melt the butter in a separate pan and gently sauté the onion and garlic till tender while the chops are browning.

3.

Cook, stirring occasionally, until the cabbage has wilted and the cauliflower is tender, about 5 to 8 minutes. Season with salt and pepper to taste.

4.

Pour the cream into a heavy-bottomed pot and bring to a simmer to make the sauce. Simmer, stirring occasionally, until the cream has reduced by half (the colour changes slightly and the cream becomes thick).

5.

Remove the pan from the heat and add the mustards, along with a pinch of salt and pepper.

6.

Serve the chops with a side of bubble and squeak and a drizzle of mustard sauce.

SOUP WITH BEEF GULLAY

Time to prepare: 1 hour and 10 minutes

Ingredients

• 4 tablespoons butter

• 2 chopped white onions

• 12 cup carrots, grated

• 2 celery stalks, cut

• 3 garlic cloves, sliced

• 1 sliced red pepper

• 150 g minced beef

• 125 g quartered button mushrooms

• 12 teaspoon paprika

- 1 tsp paprika (smoked)

- 2 tsp cumin powder

- 2 tsp cinnamon powder

- 1 tbsp thyme (dried)

1 tablespoon tomato paste

- 1 leaf of bay

- 400 g peeled whole tomatoes, blended

- 750 mL stock (chicken)

- 12 cup sour cream or greek yoghurt

- 3 tbsp parsley, chopped

CHAPTER TWENTY-TWO

RECIPE 14

Instructions

1.

In a saucepan, melt the butter and sauté the onions, carrots, celery, mushroom, and red pepper until tender and starting to color.

2.

Sauté the garlic, cumin, and cinnamon until the mixture smells fragrant.

3.

Fry the beef mince until it is browned. Make sure to stir it constantly while it's cooking to avoid meaty lumps.

4.

Gently fry for a minute with the paprika, smoked paprika, thyme, tomato paste, and bay leaves.

5.

Simmer for 30 minutes with the canned tomatoes and chicken stock.

6.

Remove the pan from the heat and add the yoghurt and parsley.

7.

Season with salt and pepper to taste.

CURRY WITH THAI RED CHICKEN

1 hour 15 minutes of preparation time

Ingredients

- coconut oil, 6 tbsp

- 8 chicken thighs, deboned and cut into thirds

- 1 tablespoon of red curry paste

- 1 garlic clove, chopped

- 1 tbsp ginger, grated

- 1 lemongrass stalk, halved and bruised lengthwise

- 1 quart of chicken stock

- 1 gallon coconut milk

- a third of a cup of coconut cream

- 2 aubergines, peeled and diced

- 4 leaves of lime

- 125 g sugar snaps or mange tout

• 1 cup coarsely chopped coriander

• a handful of roughly chopped basil

• 1 tablespoon of fish sauce

• 1 tablespoon xylitol

• 1 lime, freshly squeezed

CHAPTER TWENTY-THREE

RECIPE 15

Instructions

1.

Preheat the oven to 200 degrees Celsius.

2.

On a roasting tray, place the aubergine. 3 tablespoons coconut oil, melted, drizzled over aubergine Roast for 25 minutes, or until golden brown and soft.

3.

Sear the chicken in a deep frying pan with 2 tablespoons coconut oil until it is nicely browned. Remove the pan from the heat and set it aside.

4.

Fry the curry paste in the remaining coconut oil for a minute, or until it begins to smell fragrant. Combine the ginger and garlic in a bowl.

5.

Allow 10 minutes for the curry to thicken before adding the chicken stock, coconut milk, coconut cream, lime leaves, and lemongrass. Depending on the heat of your stove, this may take a little longer. The sauce should be the consistency of cold coconut cream.

6.

Cook for another 5 minutes after adding the chicken, aubergines, and sugar snaps.

7.

Remove the curry from the heat and stir in the fresh lime juice, herbs, fish sauce, and xylitol. Add a little more fish sauce if you want to add a little more salt.

8.

Serve with a side of caulirice.

Omelette that has been baked

Time to prepare: 30 minutes

Ingredients

• a half-cup of heavy cream

• 14 cup finely chopped onion

• A total of 8 eggs

• Green peppers, quarter cup

• 1 pound bacon bits

• 1 cheese cup (cheddar)

CHAPTER TWENTY-FOUR

RECIPE 16

Instructions

1.

Preheat the oven to 200 degrees Fahrenheit.

2.

Grate the cheese and cook the bacon slices.

3.

To make a nice mixture, whisk the cream and eggs together in a large mixing bowl.

4.

Stir in the onion, cheese, green pepper, and bacon until everything is well combined.

5.

Spray and bake a medium-sized square baking pan, then pour the mixture from step 4 into it.

6.

Bake for about 20 minutes, or until golden brown, then cool before serving.

breakfast with chia seeds

Time to prepare

4 hours and ten minutes

RECIPE 17

Ingredients

• 12 c. chia seeds

• Water (250 milliliters)

• Cinnamon (1 tablespoon)

• coconut milk (400 milliliters)

• a quarter-teaspoon of salt

• 1 tablespoon vanilla extract

• 2 tblsp. xylitol

RECIPE 18

Instructions

1.

Combine the water and coconut milk in a mixing bowl.

2.

Warm up the ingredients.

3.

Combine the remaining ingredients in a large mixing bowl and thoroughly combine.

4.

Allow the mixture to sit for at least 4 hours or overnight.

5.

Warm the mixture in the microwave for about half a minute before serving.

6.

Serve with strawberry, mango, or kiwi slices as garnish.

Recipe for bobotie

Time to prepare

CHAPTER TWENTY-SEVEN

RECIPE 19

Ingredients

• Meat

• 1 tablespoon of melted butter

• 12 onion, chopped

• 12 tbsp turmeric powder

• 1 apple (green)

• 1 tablespoon of melted butter

• xylitol, 2 tblsp.

- Salt

- 2 tbsp. psyllium husk

- 2 tblsp almond flour

- 1 tblsp. medium curry

- 1 tblsp. of lemon juice

- Here are some of the most delectable waffle recipes to try at home.

RECIPE 20

Topping

• 3 tbsp. heavy cream

• 3 egg yolks

• 200 mL (milliliters)

• 8 oz. almonds

RECIPE 21

Instructions

1.

Preheat the oven to 180 degrees Fahrenheit.

2.

After the onions have softened, add the turmeric, curry, and mince. Make sure the mince is loose.

3.

Combine the lemon juice, salt, xylitol, butter, apple, almond flour, and psyllium in a large mixing bowl. Place the mixture in a baking dish and bake it.

4.

Pour the eggs, cream, and milk over the meat after whisking them together.

5.

Bake until the topping is golden brown, layering the almonds on top.

Vegetable medley with a Mediterranean flair

Time to prepare: 40 minutes

Ingredients

• 12 tbsp cumin powder

• 1 onion, chopped

• 3 medium-sized carrots, sliced

• 1 tblsp. extra virgin olive oil

- 1 tablespoon of paprika

- 1 pepper, red

- 2 courgettes, sliced

- 2x400 grams of tinned tomatoes

- 2 sprigs of fresh thyme

- 1 tablespoon of dried thyme

- 1 yellow pepper

- 250 milliliters of veg stock

- 3 cloves of crashed garlic

CHAPTER THIRTY

RECIPE 22

Instructions

1.

Slice all the vegetables but the courgette slices should be thick.

2.

Heat the oil in a heavy pan and add the onions and cook for about 10 minutes.

3.

Add the dried thyme, carrots, garlic, celery, peppers and spices and cook for 5 minutes.

4.

Proceed to add the stock, fresh thyme, tomatoes and courgettes, and cook for about 25 minutes.

5.

Take out the thyme sprigs then simmer for two minutes and serve.

chicken with lemon and chili

Time to prepare: 35 minutes

Ingredients

• 2 lemons

• 6 chicken breasts

• 200 grams of cherry tomatoes

• 10 grams of fresh mint

- 12 courgettes

- 2 onions

- 2 fresh chillies

- 4 fresh garlic

- South Africa crunchie recipe that you should cook at home

CHAPTER THIRTY-ONE

RECIPE 23

Instructions

1.

While pre-heating your oven to 180 degrees Celsius, slice the fresh mint and onions finely.

2.

Squeeze the lemon and set aside the juice.

3.

Place the cherry tomatoes in a roasting dish, drizzle some olive oil, scatter with mint, then roast for 15 minutes.

4.

Shave the courgettes lengthwise using a tomato peeler.

5.

Slice the chicken breasts lengthwise into 4 strips per breast then sprinkle some pepper and salt.

6.

Spray some olive oil on a non-stick pan over medium heat and when the oil is hot, add the chicken strips, half of the lemon juice, chilli and garlic, and cook for 4 minutes on each side until brown.

7.

Use a large pan to prevent the strips from overlapping and once the strips are done, set them aside and cover using a foil paper.

8.

Add the onions and oil into the pan from the previous step and cook for about 5 minutes.

9.

Add extra olive oil (if necessary), pepper, salt, and the remaining lemon juice.

10.

Add the prepared courgette strips and cook for two minutes until they soften.

11.

The best way to serve is to place the chicken and tomatoes on the bed of courgette ribbons on individual plates.

meatballs with bacon and mince

Preparation time 20 minutes

Ingredients

• 1 large egg

• 250 grams of shredded bacon

• 500 grams of mince

• Rosemary

• 1 tablespoon of psyllium husk

• Salt and pepper

CHAPTER THIRTY-TWO

RECIPE 24

Instructions

1.

Evenly mix all the ingredients in a bowl then divide into balls that fit in your palm, and place on a plate.

2.

Place the plate with the balls in the fridge for half an hour.

3.

Bake in the oven or fry in two tablespoons of coconut oil.

CHOWDER MUSSEL

Preparation time 1 hour 20 minutes

Ingredients

• 3 tbsp butter

• 250 g streaky bacon (diced) (diced)

• 2 large onions (roughly chopped) (roughly chopped)

• 4 stalks celery (finely chopped) (finely chopped)

• 3 cloves garlic (roughly chopped) (roughly chopped)3. Add the remaining olive oil to the same pan and add the onion to sauté until it starts to caramelise, then add the add the garlic and keep stirring until it gets fragrant.

4.

Add the wine and use your wooden spoon to scrape the particles loose from the bottom of the pan.

5.

Once the wine has reduced by half, add the tomatoes, olives and capers and cook them until the wine has dried up.

6.

Now, whisk in the chicken stock and allow it decrease by half before checking the seasoning and mixing in the parsley and basil.

7.

Finally, return the fish to the pan and continue to ladle the sauce over it until it is well warmed.

CAULIFLOWER, WHOLE, ROASTED JERK

Preparation time 45 minutes

Ingredients

• 1 cauliflower head (trimmed of leaves and stemmed)

• 2 tbsp salt

• 2 tsp onion powder

- 2 tsp ground allspice

- 2 tsp garlic powder

- 1 tsp dried red chillies

- 1 tsp black pepper

- 1 tsp ground nutmeg

- 1 tsp dried chives

- 1 tsp paprika

- 1 tsp ground ginger

- ½ tsp dried thyme

- ½ tsp ground cloves

- ½ tsp ground cinnamon

- 2 tbsp coconut oil (melted) (melted)

- 1 big lemon (cut into wedges) (cut into wedges)

Chapter Thirty-Three

RECIPE 25

Instructions

1.

Preheat the oven to 180 degrees Celsius.

2.

Rub the oil and jerk spice all over it until it's evenly covered.

3.

Place the head on a baking sheet and cover with foil.

4.

Cook it for 1 hour with the foil on, then uncover it and roast for another 20 minutes. It should be almost black in color.

5.

Serve with lemon wedges right out of the oven.

HADDOCK, CHEDDAR, AND SPINACH EGGS IN THE BAKING PAN

Time to prepare: 35 minutes

Ingredients

• a little amount of butter to grease the pan

• 1 tablespoon of butter

• 80 g spinach (baby)

• 100 g cheddar cheese, grated

• 4 tablespoons cream

• a smidgeon of nutmeg

• 200 g smoked haddock, chunked

• A total of 8 eggs

CHAPTER THIRTY-FOUR

RECIPE 26

Instructions

1.

Preheat the oven to 180 degrees Celsius.

2.

Using a considerable quantity of butter, grease four large ramekins, enamel cups, or ovenproof bowls.

3.

Heat the butter in a frying pan and cook the spinach until it has wilted. Remove the spinach from the heat and squeeze off any remaining liquid.

4.

Break two eggs into each ramekin and divide the spinach and haddock amongst them. Add a tablespoon of cream, a dash of nutmeg, and some shredded cheese to the eggs. Season with salt and pepper to taste.

5.

Bake for 15–20 minutes, or until the eggs are fully cooked and golden brown on top. With a squeeze of lemon, serve right away.

TOAST WITH COCONUT

Time to prepare: 15 minutes

Ingredients

• 2 whisked eggs

• 2 slices coconut banting bread

• 2 tablespoons butter (for frying)

• berry compote or coulis

• 14 cup berries (your favourite)

• xylitol, 2 tbsp

• to be served with

• 1 tablespoon of berry coulis

• 14 cup greek yoghurt (double thick)

• 6 almonds, whole and raw, coarsely chopped

CHAPTER THIRTY-FIVE

RECIPE 27

Instructions

1.

Place the eggs in a flat basin and whisk them well.

2.

Heat the butter in a frying skillet over medium heat.

3.

Soak the bread for a few seconds on each side in the egg mixture, so that the egg is sucked out.

into the loaf of bread

4.

Fry the bread until both sides are browned.

5.

To prepare the coulis/compote, combine the berries and xylitol in a saucepan and heat to a low simmer (the berries should release their own juice, so no need to add water). Leave the berries whole for a compote. Simply purée the contents in a food processor or with a stick blender to make a coulis.

6.

Serve with the coulis, almonds, and yoghurt on the side.

SQUEAKY KASSLER CHOPS

Time to prepare: 50 minutes

Ingredients

• 2 kassler pork chops, smoked

• 2 tablespoons butter (for frying)

• for the squeak and bubble

• 2 tablespoons butter

• 1 sliced onion

• 1 garlic clove, minced

• 3 cups shredded cabbage

• 100 g florets of cauliflower

• a pinch of salt and pepper

CHAPTER THIRTY-SIX

RECIPE 28

To make the sauce

• Cream (150 mL)

• 1 tbsp mustard (dijon)

• 1 tablespoon mustard (wholegrain)

Instructions

1.

To make the chops, melt the butter in a frying pan and fry the chops on both sides until golden. Each side should take roughly 5 minutes.

2.

Melt the butter in a separate pan and gently sauté the onion and garlic till tender while the chops are browning.

3.

Cook, stirring occasionally, until the cabbage has wilted and the cauliflower is tender, about 5 to 8 minutes. Season with salt and pepper to taste.

4.

Pour the cream into a heavy-bottomed pot and bring to a simmer to make the sauce. Simmer, stirring occasionally, until the cream has reduced by half (the colour changes slightly and the cream becomes thick).

5.

Remove the pan from the heat and add the mustards, along with a pinch of salt and pepper.

6.

Serve the chops with a side of bubble and squeak and a drizzle of mustard sauce.

SOUP WITH BEEF GULLAY

Time to prepare: 1 hour and 10 minutes

Ingredients

• 4 tablespoons butter

• 2 chopped white onions

• 12 cup carrots, grated

• 2 celery stalks, cut

• 3 garlic cloves, sliced

• 1 sliced red pepper

• 150 g minced beef

• 125 g quartered button mushrooms

• 12 teaspoon paprika

- 1 tsp paprika (smoked)

- 2 tsp cumin powder

- 2 tsp cinnamon powder

- 1 tbsp thyme (dried)

1 tablespoon tomato paste

- 1 leaf of bay

- 400 g peeled whole tomatoes, blended

- 750 mL stock (chicken)

- 12 cup sour cream or greek yoghurt

- 3 tbsp parsley, chopped

CHAPTER THIRTY-SEVEN

RECIPE 29

Instructions

1.

In a saucepan, melt the butter and sauté the onions, carrots, celery, mushroom, and red pepper until tender and starting to color.

2.

Sauté the garlic, cumin, and cinnamon until the mixture smells fragrant.

3.

Fry the beef mince until it is browned. Make sure to stir it constantly while it's cooking to avoid meaty lumps.

4.

Gently fry for a minute with the paprika, smoked paprika, thyme, tomato paste, and bay leaves.

5.

Simmer for 30 minutes with the canned tomatoes and chicken stock.

6.

Remove the pan from the heat and add the yoghurt and parsley.

7.

Season with salt and pepper to taste.

CURRY WITH THAI RED CHICKEN

1 hour 15 minutes of preparation time

Ingredients

• coconut oil, 6 tbsp

• 8 chicken thighs, deboned and cut into thirds

• 1 tablespoon of red curry paste

• 1 garlic clove, chopped

• 1 tbsp ginger, grated

• 1 lemongrass stalk, halved and bruised lengthwise

• 1 quart of chicken stock

• 1 gallon coconut milk

• a third of a cup of coconut cream

• 2 aubergines, peeled and diced

• 4 leaves of lime

• 125 g sugar snaps or mange tout

• 1 cup coarsely chopped coriander

• a handful of roughly chopped basil

• 1 tablespoon of fish sauce

• 1 tablespoon xylitol

• 1 lime, freshly squeezed

CHAPTER THIRTY-EIGHT

RECIPE 29

Instructions

1.

Preheat the oven to 200 degrees Celsius.

2.

On a roasting tray, place the aubergine. 3 tablespoons coconut oil, melted, drizzled over aubergine Roast for 25 minutes, or until golden brown and soft.

3.

Sear the chicken in a deep frying pan with 2 tablespoons coconut oil until it is nicely browned. Remove the pan from the heat and set it aside.

4.

Fry the curry paste in the remaining coconut oil for a minute, or until it begins to smell fragrant. Combine the ginger and garlic in a bowl.

5.

Allow 10 minutes for the curry to thicken before adding the chicken stock, coconut milk, coconut cream, lime leaves, and lemongrass. Depending on the heat of your stove, this may take a little longer. The sauce should be the consistency of cold coconut cream.

6.

Cook for another 5 minutes after adding the chicken, aubergines, and sugar snaps.

7.

Remove the curry from the heat and stir in the fresh lime juice, herbs, fish sauce, and xylitol. Add a little more fish sauce if you want to add a little more salt.

8.

Serve with a side of caulirice.

Omelette that has been baked

Time to prepare: 30 minutes

Ingredients

• a half-cup of heavy cream

• 14 cup finely chopped onion

• A total of 8 eggs

• Green peppers, quarter cup

• 1 pound bacon bits

• 1 cheese cup (cheddar)

CHAPTER THIRTY-NINE

RECIPE 30

Instructions

1.

Preheat the oven to 200 degrees Fahrenheit.

2.

Grate the cheese and cook the bacon slices.

3.

To make a nice mixture, whisk the cream and eggs together in a large mixing bowl.

4.

Stir in the onion, cheese, green pepper, and bacon until everything is well combined.

5.

Spray and bake a medium-sized square baking pan, then pour the mixture from step 4 into it.

6.

Bake for about 20 minutes, or until golden brown, then cool before serving.

breakfast with chia seeds

Time to prepare

4 hours and ten minutes

RECIPE 31

Ingredients

- 12 c. chia seeds

- Water (250 milliliters)

- Cinnamon (1 tablespoon)

- coconut milk (400 milliliters)

- a quarter-teaspoon of salt

- 1 tablespoon vanilla extract

- 2 tblsp. xylitol

RECIPE 2

Instructions

1.

Combine the water and coconut milk in a mixing bowl.

2.

Warm up the ingredients.

3.

Combine the remaining ingredients in a large mixing bowl and thoroughly combine.

4.

Allow the mixture to sit for at least 4 hours or overnight.

5.

Warm the mixture in the microwave for about half a minute before serving.

6.

Serve with strawberry, mango, or kiwi slices as garnish.

Recipe for bobotie

Time to prepare

Chapter Forty-Two

RECIPE 32

Ingredients

• Meat

• 1 tablespoon of melted butter

• 12 onion, chopped

• 12 tbsp turmeric powder

• 1 apple (green)

• 1 tablespoon of melted butter

• xylitol, 2 tblsp.

• Salt

• 2 tbsp. psyllium husk

• 2 tblsp almond flour

• 1 tblsp. medium curry

• 1 tblsp. of lemon juice

• Here are some of the most delectable waffle recipes to try at home.

RECIPE 33

Topping

- 3 tbsp. heavy cream

- 3 egg yolks

- 200 mL (milliliters)

- 8 oz. almonds

RECIPE 34

Instructions

1.

Preheat the oven to 180 degrees Fahrenheit.

2.

After the onions have softened, add the turmeric, curry, and mince. Make sure the mince is loose.

3.

Combine the lemon juice, salt, xylitol, butter, apple, almond flour, and psyllium in a large mixing bowl. Place the mixture in a baking dish and bake it.

4.

Pour the eggs, cream, and milk over the meat after whisking them together.

5.

Bake until the topping is golden brown, layering the almonds on top.

Vegetable medley with a Mediterranean flair

Time to prepare: 40 minutes

Ingredients

• 12 tbsp cumin powder

• 1 onion, chopped

• 3 medium-sized carrots, sliced

• 1 tblsp. extra virgin olive oil

- 1 tablespoon of paprika

- 1 pepper, red

- 2 courgettes, sliced

- 2x400 grams of tinned tomatoes

- 2 sprigs of fresh thyme

- 1 tablespoon of dried thyme

- 1 yellow pepper

- 250 milliliters of veg stock

- 3 cloves of crashed garlic

CHAPTER FORTY-FIVE

RECIPE 35

Instructions

1.

Slice all the vegetables but the courgette slices should be thick.

2.

Heat the oil in a heavy pan and add the onions and cook for about 10 minutes.

3.

Add the dried thyme, carrots, garlic, celery, peppers and spices and cook for 5 minutes.

4.

Proceed to add the stock, fresh thyme, tomatoes and courgettes, and cook for about 25 minutes.

5.

Take out the thyme sprigs then simmer for two minutes and serve.

chicken with lemon and chili

Time to prepare: 35 minutes

Ingredients

• 2 lemons

• 6 chicken breasts

• 200 grams of cherry tomatoes

• 10 grams of fresh mint

- 12 courgettes

- 2 onions

- 2 fresh chillies

- 4 fresh garlic

- South Africa crunchie recipe that you should cook at home

CHAPTER FORTY-SIX

RECIPE 36

Instructions

1.

While pre-heating your oven to 180 degrees Celsius, slice the fresh mint and onions finely.

2.

Squeeze the lemon and set aside the juice.

3.

Place the cherry tomatoes in a roasting dish, drizzle some olive oil, scatter with mint, then roast for 15 minutes.

4.

Shave the courgettes lengthwise using a tomato peeler.

5.

Slice the chicken breasts lengthwise into 4 strips per breast then sprinkle some pepper and salt.

6.

Spray some olive oil on a non-stick pan over medium heat and when the oil is hot, add the chicken strips, half of the lemon juice, chilli and garlic, and cook for 4 minutes on each side until brown.

7.

Use a large pan to prevent the strips from overlapping and once the strips are done, set them aside and cover using a foil paper.

8.

Add the onions and oil into the pan from the previous step and cook for about 5 minutes.

9.

Add extra olive oil (if necessary), pepper, salt, and the remaining lemon juice.

10.

Add the prepared courgette strips and cook for two minutes until they soften.

11.

The best way to serve is to place the chicken and tomatoes on the bed of courgette ribbons on individual plates.

meatballs with bacon and mince

Preparation time 20 minutes

Ingredients

• 1 large egg

• 250 grams of shredded bacon

• 500 grams of mince

• Rosemary

• 1 tablespoon of psyllium husk

• Salt and pepper

CHAPTER FORTY-SEVEN

RECIPE 37

Instructions

1.

Evenly mix all the ingredients in a bowl then divide into balls that fit in your palm, and place on a plate.

2.

Place the plate with the balls in the fridge for half an hour.

3.

Bake in the oven or fry in two tablespoons of coconut oil.

CHOWDER MUSSEL

Preparation time 1 hour 20 minutes

Ingredients

• 3 tbsp butter

• 250 g streaky bacon (diced) (diced)

• 2 large onions (roughly chopped) (roughly chopped)

• 4 stalks celery (finely chopped) (finely chopped)

• 3 cloves garlic (roughly chopped) (roughly chopped)

• 4 medium turnips (cut into1.5cm cubes)

• 3 cups fish stock (or broth)

• 1 cup cream (preferably thick cream)

• ½ Lemon (leave it as is)

• 1 whole red chilli (cut in half lengthwise)

- 1 ¼ kg black mussels (washed and debearded)

- 1 handful fresh dill (finely chopped)

- 1 handful flat-leaf parsley (roughly chopped)

- 1 pinch salt and black pepper

Instructions

1. Get a large pot up to a medium heat and add the butter, bacon, onion, celery, garlic and turnips to saute until they are soft and well caramelised. This could take 20 minutes.

2. Add the stock and let it simmer gently with the lid on until the turnips are mushy.

3. Use a potato masher to roughly crush the turnips.

4. Now add the cream, half lemon and chilli and gently simmer until the cream begins to thicken.

5. Add in the mussels and pop the lid on for about 4 minutes for the mussels to cook. They should all be open when the lid comes off. If none of them are open, pop the lid on for a few more minutes.

6. When it seems as though no more are going to open, remove the unopened ones and turf them, then mix through the dill, parsley and check the seasoning before serving.

MUSHROOM TRUFFLE SOSATIES Preparation time 25 minutes

Ingredients

• 600 g button mushrooms (halved)

• 1 cup extra virgin olive oil

• 1 handful thyme (stemmed)

• 3 cloves garlic (peeled)

• 40 ml lemon juice (juice and zest of 1 lemon)

• 2 tbsp truffle oil

• 1 pinch salt and black pepper

CHAPTER FORTY-EIGHT

RECIPE 38

Instructions

1. Get a BBQ or a griddle pan up to a high heat.

2. Soak 8 bamboo skewers in water.

3. Using a stick blender, blitz the the olive oil, thyme, garlic, lemon zest and juice and salt and pepper in a narrow jar.

4. Pour three quarters of the marinade over the mushrooms and mix them well. Once they have sucked up the marinade, skewer them on the bamboo skewers.

5. Mix the remaining marinade with the truffle oil and keep a basting brush handy.

6. Now, grill the skewers over direct heat on the BBQ or on the griddle pan. Aim for 3 minutes on each side so they end up tender with some good caramelisation.

7. Give them one final basting of the remaining marinade with a basting brush and move them to a serving dish.

8. Splash them with whatever marinade is left and a lots of salt and serve immediately.

HOBOCHOKES Preparation time 45 minutes

Ingredients

• 1 thick leeks (washed and cut into cut into 3cm cylinders)

• 1 clove garlic (cut loosely)

• ¼ cup extra virgin olive oil

• ½ handful thyme leaves

• 500 ml white wine

• 2 whole bay leaves

• 1 handful flat-leaf parsley (roughly chopped)

CHAPTER FORTY-NINE

RECIPE 39

Instructions

1. Get the olive oil hot in a large pot and add the leeks, cut side-down as well as the garlic to fry for about 2 minutes on each side until lightly brown.

2. Now, add the thyme, bay leaf and the white wine, reducing the heat to simmer and leave it to tick away with the lid on for about 40 minutes.

3. After 40 minutes, remove the lid and pump up the heat to reduce the sauce by half (with the leeks still in the pot).

4. Finally, season with salt and black pepper and stir through the parsley before serving.

5. If you're jarring them, make sure both the jars and the leeks are steaming hot when the lid goes on, to create a sterile vacuum.

KIM CHI Preparation time

2 hours 15 minutes

CHAPTER FIFTY

RECIPE 40

Ingredients

- 1 head chinese cabbage (cut into 4cm strips)

- ¼ cup salt (local and natural is always better)

- 1 tbsp garlic (roughly chopped)

- 2 tbsp ginger (roughly chopped)

- 3 tbsp srirachi (a hot Thai chilli sauce)

- 50 ml fish sauce

• 30 ml vinegar (I use organic apple cider vinegar to help with the fermentation)

• 1 tbsp dried chilli flakes

• 1 tsp sugar (up this to 2 teaspoons sugar for an extra-sour kimchi - it ferments, don't worry)

• 12 small radishes (finely sliced)

• 4 large spring onions (chopped)

CHAPTER FIFTY-ONE

RECIPE 41

Instructions

1. Place the Chinese cabbage into a large bowl and cover it with salt, ensuring all the pieces are evenly coated.

2. Add just enough water to cover cabbage and weigh it down with a plate or smaller bowl to ensure all the cabbage is immersed in the water.

3. Soak for 2 hours.

4. Rinse the cabbage under clean running cold water until all the salt is washed away. Squeeze any excess water from the cabbage

5. Mix all the other ingredients except the radishes and spring onions and rub into the cabbage, trying to ensure even distribution.

6. Add the radishes and spring onions and mix well.

7. Press as tightly as possible into a jar with a tight-fitting lid to compress the ingredients. The tighter the better, as you want as little air in the jar as possible.

8. Seal and open every few hours and press further down – the liquid will increase as the cabbage weeps – this is the good stuff so don't throw it out!

9. Leave at room temperature for at least seven days, after which you can refrigerate.

CAPRESE SALAD WITH LOW NET CARB

Preparation time 10 minutes

Ingredients

• 4 crazy ripe roma tomatoes (sliced into 2 cm slices)

• 2 balls buffalo mozzarella (sliced into 2 cm slices)

- 1 handful basil leaves

- 4 tbsp basic vinaigrette

- 1 pinch salt and black pepper

CHAPTER FIFTY-TWO

RECIPE 42

Instructions

1. On a large serving platter, arrange the tomato, mozzarella and basil leaves by alternating and overlapping them

2. Season with salt and pepper, splash it with the vinaigrette and serve.

CHICKEN CASSEROLE WITH CASABLANCA CHICKEN

1 hour and 10 minutes to prepare

Ingredients

• 8 chicken thighs bone-in, skin-on

- 3 cloves garlic (chopped)

- 1 ½ tsp smoked paprika

- 1 ½ tsp ground tumeric

- 1 tsp whole cumin seeds

- ¼ cup extra virgin olive oil

- 2 medium onions (chopped)

- 2 cups chicken stock

- 1 large lemon (thinly sliced)

- ½ cup green olives (pitted)

- 1 pinch saffron strands

- 1 handful fresh coriander (chopped)

- 1 pinch salt and black pepper

Chapter Fifty-Three

RECIPE 43

Instructions

1. Blend the garlic, paprika, turmeric, cumin seeds, some salt and half the olive oil in a food processor into a smooth paste.

2. Massage the paste into the chicken pieces and leave them to marinate for 4 hours

3. Heat the remaining olive oil in a large pan and add the onions and chicken thighs to cook on each side until golden-brown.

4. Then, add the stock (and enough water to reach halfway up the chicken if needed), the lemon slices, olives and saffron and bring it to a simmer.

5. Leave it to simmmer uncovered for 30 minutes, then stir through the coriander, season with salt and pepper, and serve.

SEED CRACKERS Preparation time 20 minutes

Ingredients

• 100 g sunflower seeds

• 100 g pumpkin seeds

• 60 g flaxseeds

• 100 g sesame seeds

• 3 tbsp psyllium husks

• 400 ml water

• 1 tsp salt

CHAPTER FIFTY-FOUR

RECIPE 44

Instructions

1. Preheat your oven to 150°C. If you have a fan oven, make sure the fan is on.

2. In a mixing bowl, combine all of the ingredients and leave the mixture to stand until it is thick and pliable, about 10 or 15 minutes.

3. Spread the mixture out as thinly as possible on a baking tray lined with a silicone mat or baking parchment (silicone paper). You may need two trays. The mix should have no holes in it.

4. Bake the trays for an hour, checking them every 15 minutes. You may need to rotate them

away from the hot spots in the oven.

5. They usually take about 1 hour 20 minutes to cook. Once they are lightly browned and crisp take them out of the oven and leave them to cool.

6. Once cooled, break them into any size you like and store in an airtight container.

BAKED CHILLI CON CARNE – OR SIMPLY 'CHILI'

Preparation time 2 hour 35 minutes

Ingredients

• 600 g stewing beef (chuck - cut into 3cm cubes)

• 2 tbsp chilli powder

• ½ tsp cayenne pepper

• 1 tbsp whole cumin seeds

- ¼ tsp ground cinnamon

- 1 tsp dried oregano

- ½ tsp black pepper

- 2 tsp salt

- 1 tbsp extra virgin olive oil

- 1 medium onion (chopped)

- 2 stalks celery (chopped)

- 2 cloves garlic (chopped)

- 1 whole jalapeño chilli (seeded and chopped)

- 1 tsp tomato paste

- 1 cup beef stock (or broth)

- 400 g tin chopped tomatoes

- 2 whole bay leaves

- ½ handful coriander (chopped)

- ½ handful flat-leaf parsley (chopped)

- 2 medium spring onions (chopped)

Chapter Fifty-Five

RECIPE 45

Instructions

1. Preheat the oven to 160 degrees Fahrenheit.

2. Combine the meat, chili powder, cayenne pepper, cumin, cinnamon, oregano, bay leaves, pepper, and salt in a large mixing basin.

3. Heat the oil in a big pan over high heat and add the meat cubes. Only enough to cover 34% of the pan's base. They won't brown well if you don't do this.

4. Cook the beef cubes until dark brown on both sides, then repeat with the remaining cubes and put aside.

5. Add the onions and celery to the same pan and cook until tender, then add the garlic and jalapenos and heat until fragrant.

6. Finally, bring to a boil the meat, tomato paste, beef broth, diced tomatoes, and bay leaves.

7. Pour everything into an ovenproof dish, cover it with foil (or simply the lid if the pot is oven proof), and bake it for 2 hours.

8. Remove the cover after 2 hours, toss in the herbs, and top with spring onions before serving.

serving. With a dollop of sour cream and a touch of fresh lime, this dish is perfect.

CUCUMBER SALAD WITH SPICY KOREAN INGREDIENTS

Time to prepare: 20 minutes

Ingredients

• 1 cucumber (English) (halved, seeded and thinly sliced on the diagonal)

• 1 medium brown onion (12 oz) (thinly sliced)

• 1 spring onion, medium (thinly sliced)

• 1 carrot, big (julienned)

• 2 garlic cloves (minced)

• 2 ginger thumbs (grated on the microplane)

• 1 tablespoon (tbsp) fish sauce

• 1 tablespoon of gochugaru (Korean hot chilli flakes)

• 1 teaspoon of salt

RECIPE 46

Instructions

1. Sprinkle the cucumbers with salt and let aside for 30 minutes to sweat.

2. Now, rinse them, wipe them dry, and combine them with the onion, spring onion, carrot, garlic, ginger, fish sauce, and gochugaru in a mixing dish.

3. Refrigerate for 24 hours before serving.

RECIPE 47

CABBAGE WEDGES SPICY ROASTED

Time to prepare: 1 hour and 5 minutes

Ingredients

• 12 cabbages (cut into 4 wedges)

• 4 tbsp olive oil (extra virgin)

• one garlic clove (minced)

• 4 tomatoes that have been sun-dried (finely chopped)

• 14 tablespoons dried chili flakes

- 1 tblsp mustard (dijon)

- 12 tblsp basil (finely chopped)

- 12 tblsp parsley (finely chopped)

- 1 tsp. black pepper and 1 tsp. salt

CHAPTER FIFTY-EIGHT

RECIPE 48

Instructions

1. Toss the cabbage wedges with the dressing in the dish and place them on a baking pan, saving any remaining dressing.

2. Cover the tray with foil and roast for 40 minutes, then remove the foil and return them to the oven for another 15 minutes to crisp up and brown.

3. Remove from the fire, return them to the mixing bowl with the herbs and any remaining dressing, and toss well before serving.

30 MINUTE PREPATION TIME FOR LOW-CARB TUNA POKE BOWLS

Ingredients

- Cut 800 g fresh tuna into 2.5cm cubes

- Sesame oil (100 mL)

- a quarter cup of soy sauce

- 3 tablespoons lime juice

2 tablespoons rice vinegar

- 2 tbsp coarsely grated ginger

- 1 cup pineapple, diced

- 2 cups red cabbage, shredded

- 2 cups big English cucumber cubes

- edamame (1 cup)

12 CUP SPRING ONION, FINELY CRUMBLED

- 2 cups avocado cubes

- 2 tablespoons red chilies

- sesame seeds, 2 tbsp

Instructions

1. Combine the tuna, sesame oil, soy sauce, lime juice, rice vinegar, chili, garlic, and ginger in a large mixing bowl and set aside for approximately half a day. At the very least, one hour.

2. To serve, combine the remaining ingredients in a large mixing bowl, except the sesame seeds, and distribute among four serving plates.

3. Finally, place the marinated tuna on top of each dish and sprinkle with sesame seeds.

CPSIA information can be obtained
at www.ICGtesting.com
Printed in the USA
LVHW061327070422
715596LV00006B/122